GOOD KARMA

GOOD
KARMA

❖

Kaitlin

To order additional copies of this book, contact:
Xlibris Corporation
1-888-795-4274
www.Xlibris.com
Orders@Xlibris.com
31939

dedication

to all those whom have loved me along the way

There are no mistakes, only lessons not yet learned.

Karma is ubiquitous, affecting every facet of our lives. It is always good in the sense that it connects us to one another and to our spirits and souls. All karmic lessons help us learn what we need to learn. There are many karmic paths and always choices within them.

Karma can be found at the root of every causality; every joy and difficulty. We need to seek to understand why we are experiencing life in a way that feels beautiful or dissatisfying. We look to ourselves, for we have only ourselves to blame, or to give approbation. We can take the responsibility for changing the situation or choosing to continue on a positive path.

The one constant of karma is that it is always changing and evolving. Every action, conversation and thought affects our karma, and when we are on a good karmic path, life is facile. Our energy seems to naturally flow as we feel guided.

It is goodness, truly being loving that brings us good karma. To truly love is shown by sharing the hopes, wishes and dreams of another. It involves trust in relationships, including the one with ourselves. It is also evident when we have respect for our own desires, as well as those of others. To have faith and compassion brings us into the light and our spirits and souls will be wholly full of life and love.

It does take work to better ourselves, and to attain good karma. If we are complacent, we will continue with the same ideas, ideals and manner in which we see the world. However, if we desire success, complacency will not help us to achieve our dreams. The most important lesson to remember is: when our lives are not going well, we need to go with the flow and try to understand our karma. If we seek not to fight, we will find peace within.

Self-esteem is also an important element of karma. How we feel about ourselves and the power of those beliefs cannot be underestimated. If our faith is great enough, what we wish to happen can be brought into our lives. Conversely, if we expect bad karma, then that, too, can be carried into our lives.

Lessons learned whether from our spirits, souls or others help to move us to a better place. These lessons can manifest themselves in all manner of ways. Seeking to understand assists us in gaining good karma. We become more sensitive in this way, in particular to the needs of others, as well as to our own needs.

Communing with others, through conversation or comfortable silences where there is no need for words also brings us good karma. Being with others helps us to become part of the world family. When we are on a good karmic path, we treat others with love and respect and find our world a joyful place to be.

Loving comes from deep within. It is this that can alter our lives more than any other feeling or experience. When we love, we are fully in the flow of life. By opening ourselves to this feeling, we will blossom as a flower does in sunlight.

Communing with our spirits and souls can guide us in our decisions. They are always accessible, and fascinating. As we search for our spirits and souls, we call them hither and find in them, ourselves. They are our creations and answer to our call.

There is always hope. Hope for ourselves, hope for others, and above all, hope for our Mother Earth. We may find ourselves in situations where there seems to be no solution. If we do not despair, and instead open ourselves to all possibilities, we find our way to clarity.

On the path of good karma, we experience all our feelings in their depth. Our openness allows us to examine every thought and experience. We are able to accept criticism and praise, without being swayed by it, and also to listen to all suggestions. By closing off no avenue, we make well informed decisions. We are inspired, and to these ideas we need to listen.

When we have good karma, our sense of humor is fully present. We find life interesting and amusing because we are so attuned to ourselves and to others. We seek to bring this joy into the lives of others by sharing our love. We laugh easily and see the silver lining in every situation. This makes us a great deal of fun to be around, and others are naturally drawn to us.

When we are on a good karmic path, mistakes are easily corrected, as the lessons are easily learned and rarely need to be repeated. We see clearly the path ahead of us, finding ourselves making all the correct choices.

Forgiveness is a gift we give to ourselves, as well as to others. It is a freeing and wonderful feeling. To forgive another for a perceived or actual wrong requires an understanding of them and their actions or words. To forgive ourselves is to truly let go of the past, so that we are fully free to live in the present moment.

Tears, as with all emotions, bring about good karma. Crying brings healing. Ourselves, our spirits and souls can be hurt, and crying allows us to release the pain. Thus, we begin to heal. However, we cry for reasons other than sorrow. Joy also can bring tears; we may cry over a kindness shown, or the beauty of another being.

Freedom is another step along the path of good karma. Thus, we are able to enjoy the benefits of love and life. We are free to laugh, free to cry and free to be ourselves. Good karma brings us these gifts.

By allowing life to unfold, grace can enter our lives. We are accepting of what is, and once we have accepted another or ourselves, we are free to change. All things do change and by understanding our karma, we become free to be ourselves.

In order to have good karma, we must have faith. Not only do we have faith in ourselves, but our spirits and souls have faith in us as well. Sometimes, having faith in others can begin us on a good path. Alternatively, having someone in our lives who has great faith in us, can create faith in ourselves.

It is always wise to take time for ourselves and meditation can be extraordinarily helpful. It allows us to get to know ourselves, and also assists us in understanding karma, ours, as well as others. We are therefore better able to see our choices and thus make wiser decisions.

On the path of good karma our thoughts are clear, forever seeing the possibilities in our world. These possibilities take time to come into fruition, and therefore, should be given free reign to develop.

Possibilities can become dreams. It is important to dream, and to allow those dreams to guide us ever higher. The stronger our dreams, the greater the possibility that they will be realized. Our dreams seem possible, even probable, as we walk this path. We reach for the stars, and find that they are easily captured.

Relationships come easily when we have good karma because we feel entirely free to be ourselves and truly expressive. We are able to give freely, expecting nothing in return. We naturally feel faith in others, as well as love towards them. These relationships need to be nourished and tended. This love is returned, as it is given as a gift. For love is a gift.

Friendship also brings about good karma because it is through those whom we love that we truly learn the most about ourselves. We can give of ourselves, and also receive the gifts that friendship brings. True friends are always there for us, whether it is just a sympathetic ear or a shoulder to lean on. Being a friend to others brings such joy into our lives.

Being grateful is a beautiful emotion. Gratitude for what we are and have in our lives is a glorious manner in which to celebrate life. It causes us to be humble towards others and our surroundings. There is always something for which to be grateful.

Others trust our decisions and judgment, as we are fully able to look at all sides of a question. This comes from wisdom and patience. Thus, we are sought after for advice and counsel. We help our friends to develop their own good karma, as we guide them along the path.

On a good karmic path, the sense of excitement that surrounds us is contagious. We seem to float along, as life goes our way. However, it takes not only work, but courage as well to remain on this path. To face our fears, and feel faith in the good occurrences that are sure to follow assists our fears in subsiding, allowing us to be more free.

It is important to remain faithful to our ideas and ideals. We never compromise our integrity, honoring our promises and vows. Those promises and vows that we make to ourselves, are just as important as those we make to others. This creates personal integrity.

When we have good karma, we are able to envision reality the way we wish it to be. Our vision comes easily, and it is important to take the time to allow these visions to develop into reality. We feed them our energy and love. Creation is a process, and thus needs to be nurtured.

Empathy and sympathy also play a large role in having good karma. Being able to have compassion towards another being or creature is a beautiful feeling. We feel compassionate in all situations, never pausing to contemplate what gain for ourselves the experience will net.

Karma is a complex web of wonders that is woven through our lives. These webs may create a pattern when we are relearning a lesson. Thus, it is wise to pay attention to these patterns for it indicates that we are having an experience from which we have already had a chance to learn. We need to listen to these lessons, for they may be the ones that affect us most deeply.

Realness is another important step on this path. It shows in all relationships, even with ourselves while on a good karmic path. We are attuned to our feelings and can express them clearly. We are free to be ourselves and consequently, we become free.

Authenticity comes in a large part from being truthful. The more truthful we can be with ourselves and with others about our feelings, the greater our realness becomes. This allows for closer relationships with others or with ourselves.

Happiness is another demarcation of this path. It requires little effort to laugh, to love, and to feel connected to others. We experience sorrow and pain as well, yet it is best to be honest about our feelings, not seeking to rid ourselves of them. When we experience our feelings in all their depth, we will find peace.

Faith in the compassion of others is beautiful, to truly have an interdependence with humanity. While it is well to count on ourselves, allowing others to help us is a sign of faith. Belief in the love and dreams of others and humbleness to them can lead to true learning. We then realize that we are no longer alone and instead, we are part of the world family.

It is not true that we need to love ourselves before we can love another. Oftentimes, self-love comes through loving others, or feeling loved. This feeling exudes so that others around us are drawn into these feelings as well. We feel secure in the love from our spirits and souls, our love for ourselves and others.

Love can heal many wounds. It makes our hearts whole, and brings peace to our soul. It can bring joy to even the saddest heart. It helps us to shine and to be fully present. A smile comes easily as we unselfishly give of ourselves to others, and find the rewards great.

Being humble is a very important facet on the path of good karma. It can be humbleness towards another human being or towards our spirits and souls, in awe of their love and knowledge. This humbleness can be demonstrated through an ability to laugh at ourselves and to find humor in the most difficult of situations.

As our dreams begin to materialize, we have a greater sense of self. Our spirits and souls believe in us, as do others, because our belief is contagious. Truly believing in our ability to grow in a spiritual and soulful nature, and to be good caretakers of our Mother Earth are qualities of this path.

When we have good karma, we truly know and trust ourselves. We trust our decisions as well as our feelings because we are closely attuned to them. We have faith in our goodness.

When we have good karma, we know our fellow humans as a family. We all share the same home, and we are Her caretakers. Joining with others to make this a better planet, in whatever manner we are able, assists us in growing closer to our communities, both locally and globally.

When we are on a good karmic path, we allow others to be themselves. They are at their best in these circumstances; we can see them as they truly are. This may be positive or negative, however, we are able to handle any situation.

A kindness shown to another creature brings us joy and a sense of peace. This can be accomplished by being emotionally and physically there for a friend, or by giving of ourselves to a complete stranger. Kindness, like all karma, is returned and helps us to feel the care of others.

Joy in life brings good karma. To take pleasure in the most simple of activities, as well as the momentous occasions, brings a sense of happiness and well being. This feeling emanates from us to others, bringing joy into the lives of others.

Each success builds upon itself, bringing us more fully into a state of good karma. Our spirits and souls are full, whole and balanced as they and others guide us along the path. Taking all things to their natural completion or fruition is important. Let us follow our dreams as far as they will take us.

Printed in the United States
86420LV00004B/343/A

9 781425 701673